LUCKIER THAN THE STARS

Poems
by
Helga Kidder

BLUE LIGHT PRESS ✦ 1ST WORLD PUBLISHING

1st WORLD
PUBLISHING

SAN FRANCISCO ✦ FAIRFIELD ✦ DELHI

LUCKIER THAN THE STARS

Copyright ©2013 by Helga Kidder

1ST WORLD LIBRARY
809 S. 2nd Street
Fairfield, Iowa 52556
www.1stworldpublishing.com

BLUE LIGHT PRESS
www.bluelightpress.com
Email: bluelightpress@aol.com

BOOK & COVER DESIGN
Melanie Gendron

COVER ART
Lauren Kidder

AUTHOR PHOTO
Everett Kidder

FIRST EDITION

LCCN: 2013943055

ISBN: 978-1-4218-8669-5

Acknowledgements

Alabama State Poetry Prize — O'Keeffe's Purple Petunia

Blue Light Press Anthology: Night, Epiphany—

Chug — Fallen Angels

Conches — Borders

Common Ground Review — Transition

Free Focus — Judgment Day

Handful of Dust — Night

Louisville Review — 2618 Glenwood Parkway, Racing to the Moon

Mademoiselle's Fingers —Picasso's Blue Nude

Phoenix — Intersections, This is the Road to Somewhere

Sugarmule.com — The Soul

Woman Made Gallery — Rooms by the Sea

Heart Rhythms: Anthology — Playing with Fire

The Poetry of Relationships: Anthology — Letter from My Daughter

Relationships and Other Stuff: Anthology — Watching you Get a MOM Tattoo

Southern Light: Anthology — Judgment Day, Movement in Four Sections, Room by the Sea

Libba Moore Poetry Prize — Still Talking

Patricia Parnell Poetry Prize — The Kiss

Some of these poems had previously different titles and appeared in different form.

Table of Contents

2618 Glenwood Parkway   1

I. After the War

Summer Shadows   6
Children Should Be Seen Not Heard   7
O'Keeffe's *Purple Petunia*   8
Transition   9
Morning Rain   10
Still Talking   11
Awakening   12
Racing to the Moon   13
Maidengrass   14
Movement in Four Sections   15
Muse   16

II. Marriage

Truce   18
Seven Moons   19
Picasso's *Blue Nude*   20
Liebestod   21
The Kiss by Gustav Klimt   22
Alarm   23
Borders   24
Meditation on St. Simon's Island   26
Rooms by the Sea   27
Fallen Angels   28
Playing with Fire   29
After the Fall   30
Concerto   31
The Soul   32

In the last Century 33

Intersections 34

Winter Solstice 35

Stone Soup 37

Sometimes when you sleep 38

Selvage 39

III. When nothing is given, all things remain invisible

Sunday's Child 42

A.D.H.D. 43

Match Point 44

Thursday Morning Bouquet 45

Sixth Grade Graduation 47

Letter from My Daughter 48

Eclipse 49

Juvenile Court Waiting Room 50

Plastic Flower 51

This is the Road to Somewhere 52

Object of Art 53

Watching You Get A MOM Tattoo 54

Day Before Thanksgiving 55

Wildlife Cited 56

Renovation 57

Predestination 58

IV. When words like men look alike

Night 60

Epiphany 61

Endangered Species 62

Evening Storm 63

Falling 64

Judgment Day 65

Stardust   66
Sinfonia   67
Bridges   68
Anatomy Lesson   69
Tapestry   70
Three Fires of Spring   71
Opening   72
How to Hold On   73
After Reading Nothing Daunted   74
Seal Rock   75
Celebrating Mexico's Freedom   76

About the Author   77

2618 Glenwood Parkway

If you jimmied the warped sash
of that second story casement window,
you'd be breaking and entering
into the beginning of my American life,
now a 40-year memory.
Every time I drive by the apartment,
I want to slam on the brakes
of its paint-peeling past.
You'd find me at first
not speaking English, unable to explain
to you or anyone else the final light
green of surrounding oaks
as the sun crawled each day over them
and into the night, but twisting
with Chubby Checker on TV, mimicking
American girls who stroke their teeth
and remove unwanted hair
with *Nair* or an electric razor,
girls whose eye shadow traps the sky.
Sometime later, you'd catch me
eating a Colonial bread sandwich,
baked one day longer, though I never understood
why that was necessary. Prying further,
you'd soon know I continue to dream
in German, asking Mother's advice
on weighing fine flour and baking sweet cake
with salted butter, asking the meaning
of packages labeled as pitted and unpitted prunes.
She'd always answer,
never refuse yourself to your husband.

But I could understand neighbors'
gestures, smiles, hugs, the obligatory
shaking of hands, the shrugs
and let American life vibrate in me, swing,
like the freedom of a traveling salesman husband,
a free country. Rummaging
through my dresser drawers, you'd also discover
I'm writing home to tell them
that my Finnish neighbor named
her baby girl *Tuna*,
which, though odd, is another expression
for freedom.
Anything is okay: A baby-blue mohair pullover
over pink stretch pants, the neighbor's
white leather upholstery, swaying
in the swing on the playground, shimmying
with teenagers but refusing popcorn
because of its salty taste.
Everything is *okay*.
Even the curtains I'd sewn
flushed with the park's luminescence
after a rainy spell.

Eventually the curtains faded
like my American life,
waiting between Saturdays
for my husband's return home.
The obligatory German cooking,
dark, heavy gravies ladled
over dumplings and roasts,
the polishing of silver and shoes,
the baskets of laundry hauled
to the basement washer,
watching dancing shirts and sheets
through the second story kitchen window.

Sunday's hike around the ironing board
reminded me of home.
Mother had prepared me for this,
but I didn't know
I would always have to take smiles and hugs
from my neighbors, simple American families
with their backyard picnics,
roasting sausages dipped in syrup,
husbands damp-mopping vinyl kitchen floors,
husbands adoring their wives.
Yes, if you broke into the apartment,
you'd understand how I always had to steal
love from those around me
in order to write home with news.

1.

AFTER THE WAR

Thursdays the farmer
banged the front door knocker twice.
This week serpent roots,
dark in a paper sack. Mom
slivered and served survival.

Summer Shadows 1952

No trees, no flowering shrubs,
just ruined houses and dust.
Each day we asked our mothers,
how late will you polish silver
and wash for the French?

Lottie and I in cotton shifts,
out-maneuvering the boys in soccer.
She never talked about her father
deserting the front. Once, we rattled
the prison gate till the guard came.
We saw how the bricks walled up
the inside, shouted his name.

Each dusk fell into the gutters
as other mothers called,
locked doors and shuttered windows,
kept families together.
Soon smells of cooked cabbage
and potatoes tightened around the houses
and shadows leaned in, turned
what was familiar *unheimlich*,
hurried me to our one room flat
under the pitched roof.

Waiting for mother I sat at the lit table,
back against the wall, watched
the window go so dark
I could see myself in it.
Only the clock behind me
knew how long.

----
unheimlich — sinister

Children Should Be Seen
Not Heard

As a child, I harbored words,
folded each into soft cloth
like glass figurines,
their clear outlines
duplicating the dark,
burning deep
as they repeated themselves.

So when mother died,
her mouth gaping
as if the last word still stuck there,
the hinge of my mouth loosened.

Words broke, pushed free
until syllables, sentences danced
onto white space
that begged me to fill it
with language
buried for decades.

Fragments
imprisoned too long
had to be molten,
blown into new form.

O'Keeffe's *Purple Petunia*

Look at the face of this bloom.
Night in her darkest finery.
Those shadowy eyes,
hollows
preserve memory:

Mother's last request:
I rubbed her soles with spirits
so she could slip
away
quieter than a pocket door.

Forced
through another passage,
another birth,
in darkness
light knocked at my throat.

Transition

The day the box was delivered,
we took it in.
Where should we place your ashes?
The dinner table's catch-all
for deliveries seemed inappropriate.
The garage, too loose
for a formal occasion. The closet,
a small private room,
seemed perfect for you to gain
your composure among worn,
well-known dresses, skirts.
There you could still feel
you belonged, though we believed
other powers were now in play.
We fastened the closet door tightly.
We did not want to be tangled
in the jungle of clothes,
where the lion's roar echoed,
where the wave-tossed boat splashed the shore.
We did not want to meddle
in the trial and judgment of other worlds.

Morning Rain

At the funeral home, the muscle of laughter bursts
through another room's open door,
sweeps hallway floorboards,
unbalances our pirouettes of grief.

Our chatter treads lightly,
gains sparkle like a faceted diamond
held into the light,
then bends and knuckles under.

Dozing in the corner, memory stirs,
slips on walkers.

Rain streaking pollen-riddled windows
either floods or soothes.

Still Talking

This poem thinks it is my mother
offering a piece of her mind,
though I know she rests peacefully
in her urn in a niche in a wall.

Nothing like the Great Wall
measuring China for centuries,
just an erect marble slab defining
a few lives, its niches closed
with engraved plates.

I want to place
a rose into her bone vase,
to keep her Oriental rug as foot warmer.
Instead, she wants to knead
yeasted dough into her pastry board,
duplicate her urn's cross
over the loaf to rise.

As always, I listen, but she hears
the orange-breasted warbler
outside my kitchen window,
now wishing to rise and fly.

Like a child, I sit on her lap again,
smack kisses on both cheeks.
She wants the love, yet opens
the sash and wide-eyed, I blink
into the steamy billows
of transcendence, then wipe
the soot from my eyes.

Awakening

Deep in the embrace of the dead
you stir toward your betrothed.
How do you know
if not by genetic wish?

Transport for fools
like a fine Eastern rug,
time rolled up
for the weave specialist
or the ophthalmologist
who narrows your view,
takes away the side glance.

This month's moon
antlers light through pines.
Bucks lose their horns
as cattle graze on elk pasture.

In the midst of living
you turn for approval
in the eyes of the dead,
an outstretched hand,
rivaling the day's demand,
breath cold in your face.

Racing to the Moon

St. George Island

Lights out at nine – Save the sea turtles

Decoding an owl's calls
in moon-lit woods, keeps me awake.

In German folklore, owls announce death,
like the town bell at mother's passing.
Ten years ago, why think of it now?
A friend raising a wild owl?
It sits on her shoulders,
but to survive in the wild,
she must remain enemy.

Each hour hovers in the arms of trees
at home, here in the eyes of shells.
They impatiently count time
to give or take away. Is this
why the night wears an oyster shell cap,
holds the moon like a lantern?

Lying in the dark, the past is a bell,
the present, newborn sea turtles
racing to the ocean's moon
that calls me like a mother,
come to me, come to me.

Maidengrass

A gust riffles through periwinkles
as I putter in the garden.
Adagio maidengrass
leans like memory, unearthing . . .

My sister unbraids her hair,
cants over the tin bowl
as mother's hands pour
warm water over her head.
Lather, then rinse twice.
I'm next.
Afterwards we dry in the sun.

We bend our heads,
adagio movements, as we run
our fingers through long blonde tresses.
Fillies stirred by tempests
we lift our faces,
throw manes behind us.

Winnowed by breeze,
we race with the wind
as it takes us strand by strand
to this time-worn garden.
We are older now,
unable to bend our knees.

Movement in Four Sections

I.

Grandmother's piano summoned my fingers
to sing the black and white keys,
but mother held my hand
until I took another's.

II.

His words played ring around the rosy
could not keep London Bridge
from falling down
into a pit of ashes.

III.

In the last train entering the decade,
memory is a passenger,
a melancholy of inevitable arrival.

IV.

Sky mottled blue, birdsong,
moon a hand at night.
In between, I find myself
over and over.

MUSE

. . . small swollen flames lighting my way at corners
W.S Mervin

I drink you in rose hip tea.

You pucker my mouth

like sweet sour candy.

You are quaking grass

unpredictable rhythm

a vagabond.

You hitch a ride on the only train through town

a cowboy lassoing me   roping me to dirt.

Always unsure of the nature of flames

I am marked by fire.

II.
MARRIAGE

the curve of a bowback
we take turns
to sit in

Truce

God gives us the first line;
we have to do the rest.
                    Paul Valery

How do you pin your desires on a line
without hanging dirty linens?
Mother understood:
Her best on the outside line
facing neighbors.
Intimates
always on the inside line.

Seven Moons

women need a blue moon
once in a while

a full moon comforting us,
steadying passion

a confidante, weathering
yesterday's empty arms.

women need a moon
stepping boldly into the bedroom

a mystery moon
set amidst diamonds

a moon that knows
that light relies on shadow

that understands
checking the day's scale

a moon that triggers
blood   birth

a moon that preens
mirrored in water
that pushes and pulls the sea.

women need a moon
touchable at night

telling us whatever
we need to hear

Picasso's *Blue Nude*

Legs drawn to elbows,
blues oppress
the hollow between,
curved bare back.

The morning is still
flushed after
a feverish night.
Fear of the gods
kept her from naming
the good of snug kin.
Blues chain her body
to the unspoken.

She pinned grievances
on an old-fashioned line,
forgot Southern women
wax eloquent,
I'm fine,
in conversation with strangers,
nursing mint juleps.

Liebestod

Richard Wagner's *Tristan and Isolde*

I said I wanted more blitz and thunder
in the trombones
and the trumpets, not this
languishing melody of violins,
this slow death of love,
death for love's sake.

You smile, send me ahead
through the chattering crowd
as if I were too late
leaving.

The Kiss by Gustav Klimt

Desire kneels on a bed of flowers,
jewel-strewn, shawled
by a golden cloud, a mosaic of dress
and robe. Hers flocculent and swirly,
his rectangled, bold. As he pulls her
toward him, her heart begins to beat
tiny rectangles. But his bait and switch
covers her face, the way
a tarn touches shore.
Her mouth averted still wants more
than sweet talk. She wants
circles and swirls softening his chest,
unlocking his heart.

Alarm

Someone stole the honey from your alphabet,
your denial a honeycomb's hexagons.

Someone smashed in the glass door,
spooned the sweetness into a jar,
whirled off in a van.

You were crushing ice in the blender for margaritas.
You were captured,
seduced by the spy in a book.

My neighbor vacuumed her carpets.
Your alarm didn't go off.

For years you did not check if the peal
was still silvery and true.

I bite into plain toast as the ivy hangs limp
off the loft sill, screaming
water me, water me.

Borders

Releasing the body backwards
into pool slackens limbs
as the spine presses them into duty.

The sun's hands cup my face
one last time before she lets herself fall
behind the plateau of Signal Mountain.

A peace rose hurdles the fence.
Magnolia buds hustle branches,
perfume my nose.

Will the crepe myrtle redeem itself this year,
tomato plants' golden blooms
push out a bushel of fruit?

I dive through pristine water to the bottom
for pennies, surface to the smiling shark
thermometer bobbing up and down.

Hydrilla, kudzu of lakes and rivers,
forms an impenetrable mass,
barring fish and humans.

Hovering above hostas, the little stone bird
links sky to earth. The American flag
hugs the pole and absorbs weather.

Blue sky fades to light gray.
Solar lights flicker their first flame.
Cicadas tune fiddles in the surrounding woods.

One mile below, worms tunnel
and thrive, an abundant life.
Braille of existence without light.

Soon the invisible sun gilds the moon,
forgives night's growing shadows.
Who is luckier than the stars?

Meditation at St. Simon's Island

I.

Grey-webbed residue
of kelp, empty puddles,
broken shells.

II.

White lies scurry
like stilt-legged sandpipers
through our conversations.

Black lies: Delicately laced
seaweed under water,
see-through spines on shore.

I am a lone gull
skimming
brackish water at dusk.

III.

Small crimson pearl of a shell-cut
on my finger must be a shade
deeper, larger inside.

IV.

Like a sea star
nourished by the sea,
I have never been more luminous.

Rooms by the Sea

Edward Hopper

The front door is open wide
to nothing but the rippled sea. No stairs, no shore
just blue sky and blue water. Is this how
one should feel? That there is risk outside
without a life jacket?

Inside, the open doorway shapes the morning sun
on entry floor and wall. Then the wall stops,
squeezes the eye into another room.
Its puzzle pieces: a picture hanging
above a chair, the corner of a dresser.
Light throwing shadows.

I am torn between the open door of opportunity,
the fractured life inside, the destiny of any artist.
No man lives well alone.
Neither does a woman,
life spent to fit and re-fit the broken pieces.
Outside, the sea deep, wide, and calling.

Fallen Angels

When they decide to enter our lives,
they untie their cloaks, unlock
their foggy doors and slip into our memories
in gabardines, woolens, a few silks
they find in our closets.

I gave away
ten brown paper sacks of my life
and it felt good.
No matter. It all returns
as they will do in quilted, odd shapes
sorted by color, size, flowers,
stripes, inlaid appliqué,
those mitered memory wings we pull around us
against the cold to keep us whole.

My daughter climbs the tendrils
of a Jack-in-the-Beanstalk quilt
to exchange her textbooks for her dreams.
But the shapes of crazy quilts are never repeated.
Again and again our fallen angels return
in the bindings we've grown to love,
silken eyes, velvet mouths,
those outstretched hands.

Playing with Fire

All week loneliness climbed my boots
walking snowy Vermont roads.
By Saturday night, I hiked
toward New Year's Eve and a bonfire
after the poetry reading, carried
each poem as kindling.
Climbing fir-studded, moon-silvered hills
like pre-historic hunters before me,
I searched for fire to survive.
Eager to find friends in strangers
who guarded the blaze,
I bargained for fair exchange
and a way to carry the open flame home
without getting burned.

After the Fall

View from Adam's Roof over East Canal Street
—oil on panel by Andrew Lenaghan

This could be any city.
On the horizon, remnants of a park.
Left, a bridge hanging like the Golden Gate.
Right, offices scrape sky gray
where an alien specter hovers on stilts,
the way a royal reigns over roof tops.
A water tower guards scruffy edges
of squared and rectangled tenements.
Windows, some boarded, some framed,
in flaming orange, one open to a scrap of lace.
No trees, no animals.

Below antennae-armored flat roofs,
Eve's daily temptation:
a sacrosanct box that bridges her
to actors' lives she desires to mimic
to slough off her jagged edges.
She dons their flaws like attributes,
blames Adam for anything gone wrong,
as she slips into their marriage bed
content to sleep until the stars
fade into dawn.

Concerto

A feeling inside the mind or
heaven forbid what the heart will tell me.
Tell me about *amore*, the vibrating strings,
a violin, love
you've heard or felt.

Something like this
slipping so easily from the tongue
while your hands play my spine.

A grind and glide.
We play our own concertos
a bit too loud, too staccato, conducted
by a singular touch of tenderness.
Let me praise tenderness, how its crescendo
trembles between the bones.

The Soul

She hikes between heart and mind,
up the back stairs,
down the grand staircase.

Two days ago she slipped
on leaves hiding slick slate,
now unsure of her footing.

Impatient for the bruise to fade,
she runs her forefinger across
the scar.

Waiting, she knits the hours
into ropes and ladders,
asks night to unravel the rows.

In the Last Century

French lace cinches her neck
like a noose
of daylilies, eager to bloom,
invaded by chickweed.

Her fingers tumble over pearl buttons,
uncover the river's blush valley.
His face thirsts like a rainbow
for the sun after a downpour,
hands like ivy climbing birches,
burgeoning through branches.

Upstart winds predict a cold front:
another monotonous evening meal.
Violin boughs plunge into strings
for the smallest moment of melody.

Intersections

*Happiness is not an ideal of reason
but of imagination.*
                              Kant

Would you give me your small laugh again if I confessed
I carried your book of poems on a plane to Europe?
Would you believe, opening it now, each line represents
reasons to continue my own writing?

Would it matter if I confessed
our past travels in a Moebius strip, one-sided, twisted,
returning desire continuously,
that my daughter's recent essay on M.C. Escher explained how
his creations float in mathematical structures?
Would you believe that time
off-sets everything?

Would you understand my difficulty
if I confessed
the plane's steady roar deceives chaos,
that clouds gather the sky,
that your poems open the world's transom,
that I'm the intruder
trying to carry away words like jewels?

Whichever way a plane intersects,
causes a change in the sky.
Will rain release itself
early or late?
Would you wait?

I confess, I'm not on a plane to Europe.
Desire is caught in a time slip,
glass jars piled high in the garage for pick-up.
Cruising altitude 30,000 feet above my earth,
the sky, the palest shade of blue.
White winter sun illumines and warms bare branches.

Winter Solstice

On short days memory's door
is easily pressed.
Yesterday, a ribbon of birds
tied and untied the sky.
On the sill, Jordan River stones, a cross.

Rocks limn the long shore of holidays
gathering hours like sloe —
bluish, black, and sour.
Grime stares back with weepy eyes.

Our smiles have sunken
to the bottom row of teeth.
Days collect dust.
Envy is a swallow's memory.

Tonight, the moon is a giant comma
pausing the sentences of stars.

Stone Soup

Rifling through underbrush,
we discovered the stone
between us.

I added water, onion, celery
for flavor, grains for depth.
We danced around the stone.
Simmered softly.
Gave ourselves fully.

The stone leached minerals
but could not embrace
broth, or give in to seasonings.

We slurped the soup,
licked our spoons.
The stone crouched,
could not unfurl from its core.

Pink and smooth the stone
rests on the mantle,
remembers its name.

Sometimes when you sleep,

the moon fat in the window,
I listen to midnight's echo
entering the room like light,
filling my mouth with honey,
clinging to molar grooves, narrow cells,
soothing my throat.

Sometimes I hear an owl's hollow message
as it soars above oaks and pines, dives
into shallow creeks, gnaws its way through
bramble and marsh before it bursts
and clings in droplets to the breeze.

Sometimes I remember the man and woman I saw,
and I want to wake you
because they clung hard to each other
as if they knew their fall
into the abyss was inevitable.
Winds rush, flap wings,
moan to the strains of hope
as their feet touch the hard surface of every day.

Grey clouds hang low over city streets
crowded with pedestrians, cars,
horns blasting an aria
of *The Merry Widow*.
Green lights turn red.
Everything stops
except the chant of my heart.

Selvage

Day's end on the terrace above red-tiled roofs,
above grape vines climbing,
sated with pinot noir chandeliers
so that we have to look farther
to untangle this day —
to the silvery band of the river,
green-faded hills and small valleys,
praying church steeples, and higher,
where the sun plays trump with the clouds,
trying all of her hands.
The sun is pulling threads again, you say,
an old wives' tale.
I see the day dressed in a robe,
the sun tugging strands
until it falls into the open arms of night.

III.

When nothing is given,

all things remain invisible
as tomorrow's spider web

Sunday's Child

Out of season, my crepe myrtle is blooming.
When I wished you happy birthday, you said,
Mom, this day is not only about me;
it's about you . . .

As tremors fissured the house,
the sideboard slumped.
A vase slanted carnations.
The sailing picture spilled,
broke water on the tile floor,
rushed boat, bouquet, vase.
Groaning, the sideboard pushed the boat through.

As the boat grew, boards warped,
cracked doors and windows.
Rains carried the vessel
through breakers, wailing.

Birds wall-papered light.
Wind blew lavender words.

Carnations turned green.
Rainbows ribboned the sky.
The moon a nub of chalk.

A.D.H.D.

You draw wheels of a bike,
or bird's eye view:
two halves of a pineapple,
pale-fleshed, sputtering seeds.

You say this is your mind
shimmering yellow,
a street light in the dark.

You collect your thoughts
the way you scramble through woods,
dig for rocks and shards.

You reason like Nirvana in alien tunes
flailing behind bedroom doors.

Your interpretations splinter
like pieces of scrap wood
you want to nail into a swing.

Sometimes they are mice scurrying
under the kitchen table.
Even you don't know
their escape route.

Match Point

Your small frame and wiry arms,
nearly nine, force the yellow, luminous ball
over the rain-soaked net.
Back and forth, slice, chip,
as if each return could advance
my push-and-shove dreams for you,
my *Wunderkind*.

You don't understand a life dependent
on bread lines after the war,
your Oma's face carved with hope
for us to eat something solid.

As the damp settles in the small of my back,
I recall running home in the dark,
hoping Mother had returned.
Houses threw shadows like *Scherenschnitte*.
My fear our flat was still unlit
slowed my pace.

This is why I'm screaming under my breath,
through clinched teeth,
hit that ball, hit that ball.

Wunderkind – miracle child
Oma – grandmother
Scherenschnitte – silhouette cuts

Thursday Morning Bouquet

This rainy morning I hurry you
into the car for school,
away from the dog's bark,
away from a hissing raccoon treed
behind the garage, away from
your mission in life to save anything furry
in distress. It's like working wood
against the grain.

I release the engine and wipers
into a downpour that sprouts
worries about your spelling test,
the words you didn't practice last night,
my late mother's lectures planted
firmly between my shoulders.

There is no time to save a raccoon,
I explain to your pouting back,
but keep quiet about the twenty mice
that multiply in your room.

I don't know why you snicker,
why my kind words remain unsaid,
why I can't spare us this grief
growing like brambles in our heads.
Words bundle like a bouquet of mixed blooms
I will strip bare by nightfall.

Weekends you hammer wood squares,
rectangles into pet sheds,
but I doubt whether you can spell raccoon.

Our differences began the moment
I pushed your still waxy head from me
and you wailed a first sharp opinion.

All these blossoms in my head.
Blue salvias, sweetheart roses, thistles.
Tell me which one I should choose.

Sixth Grade Graduation

Fidgeting, you pipe "English Country Garden"
on your recorder for weeks, never
delivering the notes in sequence.

Blue and white uniformed,
you play in unison with forty other boys and girls.
I lean back, thank the gods for you,
your delicate face, golden-brown hair.

It seems evident now,
built up for weeks,
like scratching dirt into a garden,
that I can still teach you something:
my love,
a tight bud wanting to unfold.

Letter From My Daughter

Mom, I think it's about time that you knew
I started my period. I started
about three months ago, but I never told you
cause, well, I don't know.

If you point one arm to the North Star
and the other at the horizon,
the angle between is where you are.

Also I have a boyfriend
and have for a long time.
I have been afraid to tell you
cause you act like you don't want me to.
But I'm old enough!

No one is luckier than the stars.

I don't want to hide it anymore.
And I don't want to get into a discussion.
That's why I wrote this!

Evening red promised delight, but stars
and leaves have drawn themselves in.
Your wing beat folds in another night.

Eclipse

The year inhaled, sore-throated, sputtering.
You watch the earth's shadow
crossing the moon.

I think, moonless: A loss.
Advice glossed over recipes
in your fashion journals.

The argument between us since summer:
The company you keep
keeps you stuck in the dark.

How do we cope?

Shoulder to shoulder,
past shadows and midnight
we share the same view at the garage edge.

We are the lucky ones.

Juvenile Court Waiting Room

The sun points fingers
behind our backs
against the wall window.
We've stopped looking puzzled
at each other,
what went wrong.

An officer guards the magnetic walk-through,
yawns, leans back leisurely.
I try to read faces of names
called as they rise.

The clock's thin hands snail forward.

Have we learned how little it takes
to lose so much?
Someone ambles outside to draw
on a cigarette. To the eye,
the man, middle-aged, in ponytail,
looks more delinquent
than his boy in a crew cut.

Guilty is man-made.
You fidget. I write,
milk and bread, water plants tonight.
For now, the future is a cat
climbing our backs.
Next.

Plastic Flower

This is what we asked for:

The beginning of spring.
Bradford pears sifting the morning light.
Rain showering early blooms.

Not a plastic flower, daughter,
all stalk, rigid, green
as a dollar bill.

Yesterday, you finally turned
the key in the door
to destruction.

At drug level 3,
a Jennings 380 power
in your pocket . . .

Now, no one speaks for you
and evidence requires money.

O, little plastic flower, in our world
you have no scent. Without force
you do not bend.

Stuck in a vase,
you only collect dust.

This is the Road to Somewhere

*That's what I want to talk about; How love
of one kind or another can shape a life.*
                                        Dan O'Brien

You don't know yet
except that it takes you away
from the City of Has Been, away from
the club of dancing white powders, your friends,
and green leaves grown in the secret
of someone's home. This road has three lanes,
coming and going, traveled otherwise
by American Freightways, MS Carriers
who *deliver your future.*
An occasional foreign model
is guarded by the trees of your childhood:
Southern pine, poplar, hickory, sweet gum.
In either direction, there is plenty of land
and room for interruption and confusion.

The City of Going Somewhere is
another court of hurdles to jump without penalties.
The judges are waiting in silence.
Your sister understands.
She is steering you in the right direction
and your good sense still has the length
and width of the road to awaken soon.
You stop at a Burger King or Hardee's
for a hamburger and fries,
a salad or veggieburger for your sister.
Chew, chew, pull your heart and your God-given
talents into the future City of Being Somewhere,
which will allow you to fine tune and master.
Accept what the present time gives,
so your eyes and hands memorize
the dimensions of good intentions,
and your heart can draw them in.

Object of Art

Spanish moss slackens great oaks.
A Rose of Sharon presses
under the metal window overhang
as if something better were inside
than peeling paint and rusted hinges.

Each time she moves, she adds another tattoo
to her living canvas, as if she craved
the prick and burn, the after-sting:
Vines loop through dragons,
cursive mystic symbols, skeletons,
a torn heart dripping red down her arm.

Sidled against buggy glass,
I take stock of a neighborhood's decline,
its slow death mourned in spindly tendrils,
shriveled lawns, ragged shrubs,
broken porch slats, this heat-rash day.

Each time she moves, her voice frantic in my ear.
Summoned, I come, wish I could keep her
grounded, shove her back into the womb,
transform what has been punctured, burned off,
colored by will and time into an object of art.

Watching You Get a MOM Tattoo

Making a fist you grit your teeth
as the artist carves your arm's inside flesh,
flinch now and then.

You said, *I want to bear this pain*
in your name.

We laugh about it now.

Bold-scripted MOM above an Edelweiss,
an Alpine herb, pure and white,
worthy to climb cliffs for.

Now you can touch your pain
before your right arm moves
toward delinquency.
You can use this artifact,
this life blood given,
as arbitrator between right and wrong.

To remember many years from now
how I saw your pain written
in my name.

Day Before Thanksgiving

at the Marriott Atrium

You plunge, I walk into the pool,
you a tattoo spectacle,
your mother imprinted by years.

We small talk between
water and glass roof,
free-style and breaststroke.

My arms used to fold
underneath you so you could
learn buoyancy.

Goggle eyes and flipper fins
still wiggle you through
sky and clouds, mirrored.

We call to each other —
voices hollow,
fading.

Wildlife Cited

Listening to you tonight,
the past rose from its wood apse,
the shadows of its wings:
I keep making the wrong decisions.

I give you advice in increments,
but only old ladies mend their slippers.

The morning paper reported: *Wildlife Cited.*
Last week a coyote.
This week a bald eagle.

We continue to look at other planets.
We are encouraged that Saturn's moon
spews geysers of possibilities.

Is gravity easier on the mind?
Will bad decisions forget to slap you back,
and phone calls skip over the past,
its pins and needles?

Oh, the ramrod of decisions.
This wild, hungry life.

Renovation

At New Year's you are relieved
the small closet where you hid
is untouched,
the blurs of your childhood
inscribed in the corner,
cuneiform letters, runes,
maps of mystery,
secret roads your mind took,
language forming song on your tongue.

Your rites of becoming a teen
burns in the carpet,
cuts in the bug screen.
Glassy shards, flint, trinkets of nature,
sleep under your mattress.
Treasures I hang onto
as your voice jigs and skips
through sound waves.

Nightly our dog dances a ritual,
front paws press and carve the carpet,
hind end up, then down,
an undulating, lacy dance
until he is satisfied
and we are speechless.

Do magpies pick their territory
by how much glitter they discover?

Do dolphins trill calls to each other
so the sea is less deep and wide?

Predestination

Eager to find me in the day you were born,
your love tugs on me
the way the moon pulls on earth.

It travels a train's distance,
glides through the hours,
blows its horn,
head propped on railroad tracks,
falling asleep in my arms.

Love needs rebirth,
a pollination by hand
like the American chestnut,
fruit shiny as if polished,
pushing through split burrs.

IV.

When words like men look alike,

they are tempted to exchange meaning:
one is the firefly, the other
the light of itself in darkness.

Night

The day's blade sits
on your throat. It wants to sing

all songs. It wants
the trembling

of buds, not the nettle
stinging your out-reaching hand.

It wants the bending
into earth of meals ripened

with dripping juices
and a knife half-curled

into the needy flesh.
Only the farmer knows

how far to bring the knife
to the mouth, how to glean

food from the blade this night,
where the scarcest whisper

of the moon to the sun awakens
half the world.

Epiphany

Like Kerouac you burn for the streets
of this spring-scented city, fondle
silver-spooned rings, wooden boxes that open
to quivering bugs, hold glass beads
in a rainbow of light.

Doesn't the sky speak day after day,
uncover knowledge in the stars' alignment?
You hear the voice but only listen
when disaster's giant wave sucks you in,
then spits you back out, if you are lucky.
You listen and hear the message
but can't bear to lose anything.
Not even your contradictory self.

On good days you stand like a blindered horse
in front of a carriage for passengers
or allow yourself to be hollowed
by the world into a thin, fragile bowl.
You hunt each day to find a good deal,
a bargain, a rosewood elephant.

On good days asparagus fern and lantana bloom
below the sky, its speech, its knowledge.
This is an open door.
One foot in, you hope, is enough to change
like the movement of light
that slants the afternoon.

At night you listen to Rilke,
master of words and sentences so tight,
they take your breath.
Breathless you want to live,
to be heard.

Endangered Species

Only mystery enables us to live.
Lorca

National Geographic parades punks:
war painted, spiked hair
birds of paradise, swank in London's
Soho district.

Next page:
New Delhi beggars who inherit
sidewalk sections to sleep on.

How many have a smile folded
in their mothy woolen blankets?

My daughter knows nothing of make-do,
that love is a doorway
open only as long as it is used by a beggar.
Her bumper sticker reads: *Punks are not dead.*

Small pox, if it escapes the freezers
of our institutions, will leave the world
with another endangered species.

Virus experts relish this thought
since pox bricks, as they call the virus,
are breathtakingly beautiful

like tonight's moon-lit cricket-crazed
garden, a paradise,
where the spider spins his silvery threads,
tempting the easy fly.

Evening Storm

— for N.S.

He took the slender hand of happiness,
a *Mona Lisa*, in marriage.
You study their faces like a painting
across the dining table.

She reads his thigh
with one hand
as he turns the night's pages.

A small wind outside brushes
the window glass, opens
the fist of a leafy branch.

Love is a candle
burning the wick so slowly,
flames and words
that flicker in our eyes.

Falling

We fall for light like ripened apples.
Stick bugs cling like pine needles,
early cave figures flinted on stone.
Tiny scorpions flatten tails,
wiggle underneath doors.

A vase splays wheat
sheaves for the mantle.
Pumpkins duplicate the harvest moon
beside the chimney.
Candy corn crumbles sweet between teeth.

The mind is a butterfly,
lemon curd yellow,
winging one thought to another —
musical notes
that measure our song
as the silver coin moon
zooms in
and captures my eyes.

Judgment Day

Looking out, the tree surgeon,
hoisted to bedroom height in a bucket
like a minor god,
cuts away the years
of unchecked behavior,
limb by limb.

The crew feeds the chipper —
a thrust, grind, then a thud.

Even the dog howls.

Stardust

We are all made from the ashes of stars.

The Gulf is smooth pressed cloth
as we shuffle through shells —
whelks, arks, scallops,
curved and swirled like ears.

Beside us sanderlings forage surf
for mole crabs, screech
if we intrude into their territory.
A short-billed dowitcher skitters across
the give and take of waves.

Dolphins between breakers
swim closer, as if they knew our eyes.
Toddlers pat sand into hills and moats,
erase them with tiny pails of sea water.
Morning glory wends over dunes,
as crimson oleanders burst like dying stars.

We are created from the ashes of stars.
Our eyes patterned in waves and spirals,
thumb prints of loops and whorls.
In dreams we swoop like gulls and terns,
longings as universal as cloud formations.
Our gaze spans millions of years.

Sinfonia

Fingers blister the keyboard's alphabet
of the Sinfonia in G major
as my mind escapes through the window
exposing the afternoon's nipping wind.

Should I worry about the future
of ostrich plumes feathering the horizon
or whether a scientist explains
anthropogenic is another word
for "caused by humans?"

My journey is a wild garden,
lawn peppered with invasive clover.
Hydrangea limbs clutch the sunlight,
need staves to stay steady.

Cutworms sailed on haunches
of last week's whirlwind. Now they ravage
the buds of peonies and rhododendron.
Thick clouds churned the air.
Gales gnashed laurel leaves.

Today my mind is the sky,
crisp as mother's fresh-washed
linens on the line.
Sweetgum and sourwood waltz
to the baton of an invisible conductor.

Bridges

There was a man who wrote a symphony
based entirely on the arrangement of birds
on the power lines outside.

Cole Swenson

Cloud bridges gather storms.
Spider bridges cross branches.
Sometimes you build a bridge with a rose
bouquet, opening your arms
like a drawbridge. Hold me
before I glide like a sloop.

I think of *The Bridges of Madison County*,
how they destined a photographer
and a housewife; the *Bridge of Sighs* in Venice,
named for the prisoners
who had to cross it for their trial;
or *The Bridge to Terabithia* for two girls
whose loneliness created a magic forest.

The symphonist built a bridge with his eyes
and hands, copying birds on the page:
Line after line of black dots, some wearing
scarves, others hats. The notes
became bridges for a melody, a score
singing the world from a bird's-eye view.

Anatomy Lesson

Leonardo da Vinci concerned himself
with what the eye could see, rather
than with abstract thoughts.
Exhibit at High Museum

Leonardo compared the layers
surrounding the brain to an onion,
experimented peeling back skin slowly,
learned the spinal cord carries messages
between the brain, the organs, and limbs.

If we could peel back membranes
like an onion, could we
put a finger on knowledge?
Or should we learn to let go gracefully
what we love and can't control –

the moon,
hidden behind clouds,
an owl's persistent message.

Tapestry

The universe hangs lopsided tonight.
A gang of stars corners the left sky,
the waning moon opposes
like the thumb of God.

Is outer space as valuable as a flat in New York?
What about night sculpting ice crystals
for tomorrow's midnight sun in Sweden,
night tilting toward
a Tennessee snow storm?

The house and I sit close like old friends,
bones grating, mouths sighing
in unison. Walls sag like skin
trying to hold rooms together
for another decade.

Night silently spins a cover
over sloughed skin, thinning hair,
weaving silk to grace tomorrow's table.

Three Fires of Spring

Surrounded by sky-high oaks
and their shade-spreading canopies,
a single dogwood blooms.
Spanish moss hangs from each branch like tinsel
on a Christmas tree. As the midday sun
diffuses tree, blooms, moss,
your goddess belts out an aria of rapture.

Driving to the beach,
muscle clouds tease and seduce the sky.
One cloud pushes out his chest,
flexes his abs
like Mr. Universe,
then lounges languidly on the sky's shelf.
It is easy to love clouds.

It's been 30 years since you straddled
a bike, pushed off and pedaled.
Lifted and strong in the saddle,
you teeter past bottlebrush
purpling the roadside, a fence forsythia yellow.
You have forgotten how to steer
or balance on a pebble drive.
Aches twitch in calves and arms.
Again, you learn how weakness prickles
the small of your back.

Opening

*What is unresolved in your heart
is an opening to the mystery of your life.*
Anthony Lawler

Most days you rest peacefully on a deep shelf
of my heart's corner,
like a prisoner's uniform blending into the cell's gray walls.

Some evenings, when I watch a movie romance,
you stir as if from a dreamless sleep,
slowly lift thick-lashed lids.

You try to snatch the key from my pocket
to unlock the metal door,
but my well-trained guards spring up,
lances ready to strike.

I slow-speed the *Ode of Joy*,
sip a glass of Pinot Noir
and bury you again,
throw a lump of dirt and a single rose
into the mired hole.

How to Hold On

a train's whistle drones out dreams,
cracks dawn open

a murder of crows,
sizzling sheen, scatters screeches
through variegated leaves

virginia creeper scales claret-red
the trunk of an old white oak

the way you close out of season

snowflakes salt the hills
on stream-netted valleys, pioneers
venturing into fissures and clefts

a stowaway bee clings to my windshield,
thin legs quivering in the rush of wind

After Reading *Nothing Daunted* by Dorothy Wickenden

As a new generation covered history's lap
like a napkin,
you were a pioneer among debutantes.

You pushed through snow storms,
slipped in and out of steep crags,
scaled each day's shoulders,
to teach children in remote posts.
You called the mountains your brothers.

Like you, I've learned to dig my heels
into the frame of time I occupy,
have altered history's vintage dress
to fit my size.

Like you, I've hauled and calibrated
each rock until it was my home.

You were a peak in a range of boulders,
inscribed lines in history's schoolbook.

You hewed your own road.
I've begun paving mine.

Seal Rock

In currents that let people drown,
know who you are.

Ask to stay above the waterline.
Float your body like a buoy.

Let me hold you in your weakness.
Be nourished by clouds producing rain.

Speak to me with soft praise and thanks.
Ask for kelp, fish, and seals.

I will give you everything
you need and do not ask for.

What I want from you
neither sea nor earth can shake.

Celebrating Mexico's Freedom
in Dolores Park

Palm trees fan the wind.
The sun, a soldier battling mistral.

Lying on a blanket in Dolores Park,
      Huapango's violins fiddle
my toes. Drums pound my ears.
                       Cellos
and violas glide and chant softly
like velvet beneath violins.
                 The conductor leans
      into the rhythms
of Marquez, Chavez, Rosas.
At the finale of Mexico's *Independence Waltz*,
      she is flushed,
               breathless.

I remember my last piano lesson,
fingers trying to keep tempo
      with the *Blue Danube*,
my teacher's face
      grimacing like a clown's.
                  Anchored
in childhood's Sunday afternoons,
I huddle against the radio
      as familiar strains cut stone into facets
that memories hold against the light,
      then polish.

About the Author

Helga Kidder is a native of Germany's Black Forest region and now lives in the Tennessee hills with her husband and her dog Tyler. Her two daughters reside on the East Coast. She was awarded an MFA in Writing from Vermont College in 1994, is co-founder of the Chattanooga Writers Guild in 2001 and leads their poetry group. Her poetry and translations have appeared in *The Louisville Review*, *The Southern Indiana Review*, *The Spoon River Poetry Review*, *Comstock Review*, *Eleventh Muse*, *Moebius*, *Voices International*, and *Quiddity* among others, as well as in several anthologies. Her poetry was recently featured in *Southern Light*, Twelve Contemporary Southern Poets. She has a translation chapbook, *Gravel*. Her poetry chapbook *Wild Plums* was published by Finishing Line Press in 2012.

Thank You to Those Who Helped Make this Book Possible:

Diane Frank of Blue Light Press whose workshop inspired some of these poems and who encouraged me to bring them to press

K.B. Ballentine for her encouragement and diligent feedback on these poems

Finn Bille and John Mannone, members of the Chattanooga Writers Guild poetry group, for their feedback on these poems

My husband for encouraging my writing

Mary Kay Rummel for her reading of this manuscript and wise feedback

The participants of Open Mic for their listening to different versions of these poems

Earl Braggs for his interest in promoting these poems

www.ingramcontent.com/pod-product-compliance
Lightning Source LLC
Chambersburg PA
CBHW032027090426
42741CB00006B/757